WHAT PEOPLE ARE SAYING ABOUT

SPINNING STRAW, W...

A poetic perfection of biblical... ...with a folklore feel.
Lyn Sedmina, Christian Literature Editor, BellaOnline

Spinning Straw, Weaving Gold is a lyrical little book, rooted in myth. References to stories from the Bible and such as those of Ariadne and Penelope enrich the simple form of a dialogue between mother and daughter. As Isabel Anders says in the Introduction, "woman's work and woman's wisdom come to us...as two inseparable strands, braided within her very person," and it is in the two women's spinning and weaving that they express their wisdom, and reveal a female spirituality deeply rooted in the physical. "Work and love. Love and work. It is in the artful weaving of these two primary life strands...that deep fulfillment is sought."

The book has the tone of a conversation between guru and disciple: refreshingly recast in feminine form. Like the gold of the thread, wisdom shines through the text: a beautiful expression of woman's grounded spirituality.
Jennifer Kavanagh, Author, *Journey Home*

Isabel Anders has woven straw into gold with her wisdom-filled mother-daughter dialogues. This is a wonderful book to sit with and reflect on the treasures Anders brings that are as new as each day, and as old as the first mother and daughter conversation.

Isabel Anders is a teacher pulling up threads in the tapestry of our collective lives so that we might examine them and then weave them into our own personal tapestry.

I found myself wanting to enter into the dialogue and to be included in the conversation.

Marian Windel, Executive Director, Sophia House, Louisa, VA

Spinning Straw, Weaving Gold

A Tapestry of Mother-Daughter Wisdom

Spinning Straw, Weaving Gold

A Tapestry of Mother-Daughter Wisdom

Isabel Anders

Winchester, UK
Washington, USA

First published by Circle Books, 2012
Circle Books is an imprint of John Hunt Publishing Ltd., Laurel House, Station Approach,
Alresford, Hants, SO24 9JH, UK
office1@o-books.net
www.o-books.com

For distributor details and how to order please visit the 'Ordering' section on our website.

Text copyright: Isabel Anders 2012

ISBN: 978 1 78099 461 1

A CIP catalogue record for this book is available from the British Library.

Design: Stuart Davies

Printed and bound in the USA by Edwards Brothers Malloy

We operate a distinctive and ethical publishing philosophy in all
areas of our business, from our global network of authors to
production and worldwide distribution.

CONTENTS

Also by this author:

Becoming Flame: Uncommon Mother-Daughter Wisdom
Foreword by Phyllis Tickle

Awaiting the Child: An Advent Journal
Introduction by Madeleine L'Engle

Soul Moments: Times When Heaven Touches Earth

40-Day Journey with Madeleine L'Engle

Blessings and Prayers for Married Couples

Simple Blessings for Sacred Moments

Co-Authored with Diane Marquart Moore:

Chant of Death

Make two homes for thyself, my daughter.
One actual home...
and the other a spiritual home,
which thou are to carry with thee always.
—St. Catherine of Siena.

To all
Daughters of earth and air,
mind and memory:
Value your straw,
know and own your Gold.

Introduction

Work is love made visible.
—Kahlil Gibran.

Whether called faith, destiny, or the hand of God, slender threads are at work bringing coherence and continuity to our lives. Over time they weave a remarkable tapestry.
—Robert A. Johnson.

Woman's work and woman's wisdom come to us in literature, as in life, as two inseparable strands, braided within her very person. We are told: "The wise woman builds her house, but the foolish tears it down with her own hands" (Proverbs 14:1). A wise woman is seen in this biblical book as a builder, a tender of her household, one who works to provide for those in her care—as told of in these vibrant images: "She is not afraid for her household when it snows, for all her household are clothed in crimson" (Proverbs 31:21).

This basic, timeless biblical language offers us a thread of connection back to women's work through the ages. As an example of this vision of work and wisdom being intertwined, it is hard to imagine a more perfect example than that of Mary the mother of Jesus.

It is suggested in a legend that draws from the apocryphal Book of James that Mary as a young virgin spun scarlet thread for a curtain to adorn the temple—while Herod's architects completely rebuilt the temple around her. In this imagined scenario, the acts of spinning and weaving are brought together against the backdrop of the construction of a holy sanctuary, all together symbolizing Woman engaged in her ideal Work.

This resonant, compelling image of Mary conjures for us the "red thread" of life—a mix of blood and tears that bind together wisdom and love—here embodied in a feminine personage: the one woman who made possible the Incarnation of *Jesus the Word made flesh* himself. "She who reconciles the ill-matched threads/Of her life, and weaves them gratefully/Into a single cloth—/It's she who drives the loudmouths from the hall/And clears it for a different celebration" —in the words of Rainer Maria Rilke.[1]

Indeed, this is exactly what Mary did.

Ann Belford Ulanov wrote in *Receiving Woman:* "The receiving woman who can give abundant particularity to new realizations of ancient images is the missing element in our society. Nothing in our liturgy, as yet, deals adequately with such a being present to oneself in the presence of God as Mary offers, such a receiving of oneself, a voting of faith in human presence in the universe because God has voted faith in us first."[2]

Work and love. Love and work. It is in the artful inter-weaving of these two primary life-strands through the duration of a woman's life that deep fulfillment is sought— and often found. And it is a fair assumption that when the virtue of *discipline* is added, wisdom may be elicited and much good brought forth—with God's help.

I previously explored the vibrant image of *fire* as wisdom in my book *Becoming Flame.* I now add to it several complementary, similarly hopeful images to which women have a natural affinity. For instance, L Maloney offers this insight drawn from Jesus' parable of the lost coin, in regard to the nature of feminine theological inquiry:

"Our work is contextual and concrete; it sees the ordinary and the everyday as the place where God is revealed; it takes place 'in the house.' It is hard work; it is a struggle to find what we are seeking in the darkness that has covered it for so many centuries. But it is also characterized by joy and celebration, and by hope: a hope that assures us that God is with us. God has her skirts tucked up and is busy sweeping and searching too."[3]

Spinning and weaving, sewing "in the house," are also important themes in women's lives. The ancient art of spinning was highly valued among women's traditional skills well up until the industrial revolution. The term "spinster" survives today, usually with the negative connotation of "old maid" or a woman left to perform such a task in her parental home without the honor of rescue by a man and marriage. (Actually, the term used to refer to a single woman who was working elaborate design into her garments in anticipation of attracting a desirable husband.) In contrast, the term "bachelor" has usually been cast in a positive light through the decades, as a man having potential and a future, without reference to specific work he might be consigned to do.

The dismissive nature of the term spinster as reserved for women is no anomaly, as we see also with nouns such as "mistress"—hinting at illegitimacy (the masculine form of "master" is generally positive in connotation). Similarly with the verb "to man"—to take charge of—next to it, the potential power of the feminized form "to woman" fades to parody.

Again, the pejorative connotation of "old wives' tales" hints at possible unreliability/illegitimacy in their advice and example. Why would not the collected experience and wisdom of mature wives instead be deemed extremely valuable? And similarly, the typical image of the wise crone (usually bony, bent, with straggled locks) is never as appealing as that of the silver-bearded, commanding male wizard.

Can we then propose that the blended elements of women, work, and wisdom—and even age or endurance— be reconsidered for our time in new and fresh lights?

Today the art and craft of spinning may be making a resurgence as a creative, valued occupation for both men and women. Although the traditional hand skills of spinning and weaving have largely become mechanized in factories, individual thread- and cloth-making operations still persist, by choice, as expressions of personal art.

And we are perhaps ready for a new look at the process of spinning as a skill: the choosing of raw material for thread, dyeing it various chosen colors, building a basic framework on which to facilitate the process, handling spindle or distaff dexterously—bringing an inner vision to material reality. Such reconsideration offers the opportunity to revitalize the concept of *spinning* in spiritual terms, as a process solidly based in the good material "feel" of *work in the world that can lead to creative consequences.*

The packed image of spinning available material, redeeming the seeming dross of everyday experience and turning it into gold, weaving it into beauty, certainly derives from a practical reality. As Sally Fox points out in her beautiful illuminated book of days, *The Medieval Woman*: "Many illuminations [produced primarily in the years 1300 to 1550] show women spinning, carding wool and weaving because women *were* the textile industry."[4]

To take a raw material such as cotton or wool and facilitate the intermediate step of twisting its fiber into yarn, the long and sinewy replica of a life form (perhaps suggesting a chain similar to our own genetic spiral)—then taking this splendid medium and weaving it into representational form—has both practical and artistic aspects. The end result of a woman's weaving could be as small as a baby's cap or as massive as a castle wall's decorative covering. Large ornate tapestries were not only beautiful but also practical, serving as wind barriers to keep out the cold that permeated stone walls. Thus we can observe that beauty and function intertwined usually prove stronger and wiser than either alone.

The potential of taking this metaphor to the spiritual dimension is the possibility of inclusion, of combining, weaving, or even *braiding* several strands of available reality—and thereby preserving paradox in evocation of some of the great mysteries of *incarnate life* for both men and women.

In *Spinning Straw, Weaving Gold*, my second collection of "uncommon" mother-daughter dialogues, I focus on the wisdom to be derived specifically from women's work—which is, by definition, any work done by women. As in my Introduction to the first collection, *Becoming Flame*, I note how the overarching value of *woman's way in the world*—the slower process through which she gains experience, sifts and filters it through her natural stages of development, and eventually finds a confident voice in the world—is usually vastly underrated, and often completely ignored within larger circles of power and influence.

I proceed on the assumption that the best way to seek to refocus some of the attention that louder, brasher events command in the world is simply to give space and attention to the microcosms of women's experiences, small scenarios of lives that thrive or struggle all around us—but to see them with new eyes.

Spinning and weaving, sewing and quilting are excellent metaphors for this process that women naturally experience in their lives, which necessarily have different trajectories than men's. The story of Penelope, wife of Odysseus in *The Odyssey*, is a fitting instance of how weaving—of actual materials, or of experiences, including those of the spirit—allows women time in solitary or shared labor to evaluate, to choose, to *reflect* while creating in a slow but steady way the necessary conditions for their lives, facilitating a process through which to proceed to another stage.

In the absence of her husband on his travels, Penelope was besieged by many suitors. Yet she managed to put off selecting one who would replace her husband in the event of his not coming back. She did this by asserting that she would not choose until she had finished weaving a shroud for Odysseus' father Laertes.

For three years, she would weave during the day and then unravel her work at night, so that no progress ensued. And thus she "gained" time, the most precious commodity to the wise woman in learning how to live her life—to arrange for good the pieces of reality to which she has access.

In my mother-daughter dialogues, I envision a timeless feminine context in which not only carding, spinning, weaving, and all subsequent sewing tasks could occur, but in which two women (for the daughter has gained some maturity and works side-by-side with her mother) can actively participate in mining the wisdom that comes through their shared experience.

The line between literal activity and spiritual corollary is often as thin as thread itself. In fact, the Apostle Paul in 1 Corinthians 15:46 feels he needs to remind his readers "it is not the spiritual that is first, but the physical, and then the spiritual." And so, it makes sense for us to pay close attention to the *way* in which wisdom comes to us through our actions and experiences in the world, and specifically what this can mean to us as women.

We live and work in the world as incarnate beings. What we learn while being human day to day is the sacred ground of our training in discernment, in how to live. David Steindl-Rast has written, "This world was given to us to work on. Only in this way do we grasp the divine reality."

A Sufi master is quoted as saying: "If you put the world between you and God, the world becomes a spiritual obstacle; if you use the world to remember God, the world becomes your spiritual friend."

After the death of a beloved teacher, one of his disciples was asked, "What was most important to your teacher?" The student answered, "Whatever he happened to be doing at that moment." Saint Francis of Assisi suggested that we "Start by doing what's necessary, then do what's possible, and suddenly you are doing the impossible."

Thus, I offer these dialogues, the braiding of two voices or two strands of consciousness, with prayers that they may collectively unveil a textured tapestry of mother-daughter wisdom. And I invite you to consider how spinning *what comes to us* in many circumstances can enable us to weave something quite majestic of our lives—like straw into gold—when the spinning and the weaving are themselves the operations of love.

The Daughter asked, "How do you spin all day, and see so little for your effort, and keep from discouragement?"

The Mother answered: "See this little square of texture and design?

It is enough to wrap the universe in comfort and warmth."

The Daughter was perplexed. "How can this be?"

The Mother replied: "Even a few inches of loving intent can spread to span continents. Ask a ray of sun."

—From *Becoming Flame: Uncommon Mother-Daughter Wisdom.*

Elusive Threads

The Daughter loved the Spinning and Sewing Room, where the rough, carded wool was transformed into shimmering, useful thread.

"See," she said one morning to her Mother, pointing to the results of her effort, "our spinning teaches the wool to *connect!*"

"Yes," acknowledged her mother, "and it is our most basic lesson in life, as well, to learn how to Connect."

* * *

"I want to be present at that moment of transformation," said the Daughter, "when the airy fibers and strands of my hopes and dreams become material substance in the real world."

"By your words expressed—through the power of your desire—you have just made an instance of that very thing happen," said her Mother.

* * *

The Daughter was weary at her spinning, and reflected aloud, "What if we really *could* spin coarse straw into fine, pure strands of gold? Then surely we would not always have to work so hard."

"If you could accomplish that miracle," her mother admonished, "the responsibility it would entail would tax and exhaust you—mind and body—far beyond the demands of the quotidian tasks you have been given. How blessed it is to live a human, limited life."

* * *

The Daughter glanced up and saw a spider spinning its web in a corner of the ceiling of the Spinning Room.

"See," she pointed out as the sunlight hit the web, "how she weaves her gossamer net just above our own thread-making."

"Yes," said her Mother, "just as all creatures weave their patterns into the life of the earth and—though we often cannot even see, much less measure them—all add to the richness of Reality."

* * *

"How can Beauty age and Warmth be sold?" asked the Daughter, her eyes twinkling at the riddle she had posed during an afternoon work break.

Her Mother joined with her in their agreed-on litany:

"First Father shears the sheep."

"Then we card the wool..."

"And spin it into thread..."

"To weave it into forms..."

"Of warmth and beauty"

"And sell the shawls and throws"

"And thereby Warmth is spread—"

"And Beauty grows."

They both laughed and then resumed their stitching.

* * *

"See the spider-web design I have drawn for the next shawl?" the Daughter asked.

"Yes, it does borrow from the shape of Sister Spider's work," agreed her Mother.

"But unlike her web, we will *fill in* the spaces with our own design, to connect the threads and give it fullness," the Daughter noted.

" ...As we all must fill the spaces that the shape of our life provides us with, each in her own way," observed her Mother.

* * *

"This piece has too many loose threads..." the Daughter lamented, pulling on the errant strands. "They confuse and hinder my work."

"Thus it is our task to tie them up, as best we can, in sewing as in life. It is the doing of it that teaches us one of the ways God works with the Soul."

* * *

The Mother reflected aloud as they worked: "It is said in a mystery that 'You did knit me together in my mother's womb...'[5]—that God too 'spins' and weaves us of the stuff of life."

"I am thankful that I was 'spun' near your heart," the Daughter acknowledged quietly.

* * *

"How will I know what Work I am to do in the world when I leave our Home?" the Daughter asked aloud.

"The strands of your adult life are being gathered together day by day," her Mother assured her. "Over time you will be able to discern a distinct configuration that reveals itself, more and more, to be a Pattern."

* * *

A bird was singing its morning petition repeatedly outside the window. *"Are we? Are we?"*

"What *are* we, Mother—and *why?*—that the world beckons our ear and calls us to attention in these ways?"

"We are a puzzle wrapped in an enigma," said her Mother. "And the only 'thread' I know to follow, to find our way through life's Labyrinth, is to labor diligently while holding on to Love."

Patchwork Days

"See how these swaths of alternating sun and shadow appear in the Spinning and Sewing Room—almost like patches on a quilt," the Daughter remarked.

"And just so, we continue our work alternately in light or shadow—not only through the seasons and the days, but in stages of our lives," noted her Mother. "In observing these contrasts, we begin to perceive more of the Pattern."

"Just as my shawl is beginning to reveal how light and dark areas work together to produce a Design," the Daughter agreed, pulling at the edges of her handiwork.

* * *

The Daughter went to the pantry to choose from their supplies for the family's evening meal. The colorful, variegated jars of produce, lovingly prepared after the last harvest, stood in rows on the pantry shelves like a "calendar" of food available to consume in the year to come.

"If only I could choose the 'color' of my day as I choose a jar of food for the day's meal!" she lamented.

Her Mother walked in and put her hand on her Daughter's shoulder. "We ARE choosing," she said, "in much more subtle ways than taking down a jar from a shelf. But our hands and hearts reach out, nevertheless, and we trust that Love reaches back to us."

* * *

"I need a new dress for the Gathering in two weeks," the Daughter told her Mother. "I've grown at least an inch, and my sleeve and skirt lengths must be made to fit."

"How easy we find it to clothe the body, to make adjustments to visible changes," said her Mother. "If only we could realign our Soul as easily, when we perceive it growing in ways no measuring stick can show."

"I know that I have altered in those dimensions too," the Daughter admitted humbly.

"And I perceive those changes with my Heart," said her Mother.

* * *

"Father has built our house of many types of materials," the Daughter noted, "beam and brick, board-and-batten, stone and shingle."

"Just so," her Mother noted, "a wise woman builds her 'house' from the substances of discipline and purpose, joy and love, tears and hard work."[6]

"I want to live here with you and Father for as long as I need to learn from you," the Daughter said.

"And from these thoughts and intents of your heart, the house of your Soul grows also. Eventually it will 'house' you well, when you have gone into the world."

"But that will not be for quite a long time!" the Daughter said, hugging her Mother.

Hems and Borders

The Daughter loved to create original designs for quilts, piecing together the colors and shapes that would capture Beauty in a look, and showcase her sense of proportion and style. Yet the hemming of borders was tedious to her—the last finishing touches that made a work complete.

"Why do I so dread the final step of stitching the edges?" she asked her Mother. "It is all part of the same work—but I put it off, wishing someone else would do it for me so that I could go on to imagine new Designs!"

"Hems and borders frame the work, whether of an artist's canvas or a poem's beginning and ending. A well-stitched border teaches the eye to center on the subject, and not be distracted by undone edges," her Mother reminded her.

"Yes, I know," the Daughter answered. "And I grit my teeth and 'pay the piper' at the end of each project, as I should."

"Gradually," her Mother promised, "Life itself will teach you the Wisdom and Beauty of carefully chosen limits. You are stitching your own Soul's lessons as you tend to hems and borders."

* * *

"Sometimes in the night, when I am sleepless," the Daughter confided to her Mother, "the day's events unspool in my mind like thread peeling off a spindle."

"It is then that you are on the borders of your own rich consciousness," her Mother explained. "Such times are like perching at the edge of the intricate tapestry that is your life. Your mind can 'stand back' and view the whole more clearly."

"And the next day I can take up the threads to weave new days of them," the Daughter agreed, "full of thoughts and ideas that do not come to me in waking time."

* * *

"I feel impatient to finish today's work," the Daughter complained, pulling her brown embroidery threads through the muslin as she traced the outline of a tree, "so that I can experience the richness of filling in this Design."

"The outlines of life, the planning, the lists, the thinking ahead...all are part of the process of creating lives of Beauty, even if they do not seem so at the time."

"And so is the waiting...if only my Mind could convince my Heart!"

Circling the Square

While piecing together colored slices of material that together comprised a circle, the Daughter asked aloud, "Where is the Center of things, and how can I get there?"

"It is where Love resides, and, Daughter of my Heart, you are already *there.*"

* * *

"Mother, how will I learn to recognize Truth and make decisions on my own when you are no longer close by to advise me?"

"You will never be 'far' from me in this life or beyond it. Because Love joins us, our Souls remain connected regardless of dimensions of physical space. This is a principle of Spirit that will remind you of its Truth when you need it most."

* * *

"Who knows where we have come from and to where we go? When I think of the vast expanses of Space, I am fearful of the future," the Daughter admitted.

"The One who says 'I am with you and will keep you in all places'[7] speaks also of time dimensions. There is no 'place' where Love is inoperative. That too is a law of Spirit," her Mother assured her.

Warp and Woof

"Of what use are these leftover bits of cloth that do not fit into our design?" worried the Daughter, sifting through the pile of remnants on the sewing table.

"I have learned through the years never hastily to throw away the odd pieces and seemingly worthless scraps left from our work," the Mother explained. "Sometimes they can later prove useful and be exactly what we need."

"You have eyes to see what I cannot imagine," said the Daughter, thinking of mistakes and losses already troubling her young life. "How could these stragglings ever 'fit'?"

"You too will learn to see in this way," assured her Mother. "For now, trust me that this is so."

* * *

"The threads of our lives lead both ways—vertically toward our Source, and horizontally toward each other," the Daughter reflected, holding out her handiwork as an example.

"And the template of the Warp and Woof of life will guide you at every stage," her Mother promised. "Its applications will become myriad as you grow further into maturity. See in them the Cross, for it is the Vortex of life."

* * *

"But the threads of my own life seem weak and insubstantial, not strong enough to hold up to Life's demands," the Daughter lamented.

"Remember that our everyday choices and acts add heft

and complexity to the raw material of our lives, just as we roll and twist fiber to give it durability and strength."

"...in order to weave it into the larger Design," the Daughter finished her Mother's thought.

* * *

The Daughter was a lover of books, and sometimes had to be called from her room, compelled to pull away from the pages that delighted her and held her in thrall.

"Books are teachers," said her Mother, "but we also must learn from living people and the wider World around us. Even today, we are composing the 'sacred pages' of our lives. It is not for nothing that Meister Eckhart speaks of a right to call all creatures God's 'words.'"

* * *

"Our conversations with each other," the Mother pointed out, "are like kindling a fire—something new is ever born in the Light and Heat of them."

"And like threads intertwined," the Daughter noted, holding up colored strands, "daily we become more closely braided in strength and connection."

"And when Love attends the process, it becomes not only a conversation, but a Prayer."

Soul's School

"Mother, help decide this for me," the Daughter asked. "Am I a 'Martha,' serving by my work and attentiveness to housely detail—or a 'Mary' who listens primarily and obediently to the Word?"

"Truly, both impulses reside in your Soul, the way of *Work* guiding you when it is needed, and the thread of *Love* compelling you to follow in its own ways. You yourself need not make such distinctions. Those who have eyes to see will know you as you are meant to be known."

* * *

"Does life become easier as you increase in years?" the Daughter asked her Mother wistfully.

"At my age a woman has built her house, and her table stands on firm legs. This is a needed foundation—but each day she still must sweep the rooms, and tend the fire, and spread the board."

And her Mother did not stop as she said these things, but continued to perform the acts of Love of which she spoke.

* * *

When the Daughter came in from gathering clothes off the line, the Mother was sitting at the piano, and from her fingers a simple melody gradually progressed into the complexity of a Fugue.

When she had finished, her Daughter asked, in a riddle: "What powers the labor of our hands? Where is our work when it is done? And what is the music before it is played?"

"From the invisible drying of the clothes by Sun and Wind, we know that inscrutable, untamable forces attend us at all times. ...All that we have thought and accomplished in our lives hangs still in an Eternal Moment. ...And sometimes unheard Music is sweetest and most dear."

* * *

"I have read how great men," said the Daughter, raising her eyes from her book, "speak of 'plying' their own shuttle and 'weaving' their own destiny into unalterable threads. This sounds to me more ominous than comforting."

"The question of 'control' over our lives is one we confront every day. It is all about Balance. Too heavy a hand in any work can limit the outcome. Perhaps this is something that women can teach men," her Mother said, smiling.

Wisdom of the Unseen

"Mother, what is our trade, and how may we describe the Work of our life?"

"St. John of the Cross wrote, 'My occupation: Love. It's all I do.' We can do no better."

* * *

"I understand in principle the weaving of the two threads—the inner and the outer strands of our lives," said the Daughter. "But what of their measurement? The outer process seems to command more importance, in its visibility and material dimensions."

"But the contrast also reminds us that *what is unseen* exerts its power too. As Father says, 'Every farmer is a mystic.' Only in this Way can one respect the forces beyond our vision and learn to work with them."

* * *

"All my plans for work today have been lost in the necessities of fixing broken tools, delays, and tedious preparation, just to begin to spin!" lamented the Daughter.

"One way to express this recurring paradox has been the realization: 'For each day, there is my plan; and then there is the Mystery's plan.'"

* * *

"How much does our Work matter? We are craftspeople, and all of the Art and technique that goes into our productions is not seen or appreciated by the world."

"It is said, blessed are the molders and potters, and the weavers and handcrafters. Though they are not found among the judges and the city's rulers, they keep stable the fabric of the world, and their prayer is in the exercise of their trade."[8]

* * *

"How does the Spirit come to us—since we cannot see the 'wind' of its presence? How can we know we are being led and shown the way?"

"The great da Vinci has said, 'When the Spirit does not work with the hand, there is no art.'" Then the Mother pointed to their newest tapestry.

* * *

"In the Faery story I am reading," said the Daughter, "the act of spinning itself forges a link between the Worlds— seen and unseen. Can our physical actions thus truly bring about a bridge of knowing?"

"All Art can be seen as a borderline experience," her Mother asserted. "By it your Mind and Spirit are shaped, like the thread, toward new use and wider perception. Who is to say what worlds are right *here*, in this room, 'thin places' able to be entered by a furtive glance of Sight, or an inner assent to Love?"

* * *

"I will know, when I enter these Ways, that you, before me, have already seen the Path," the Daughter said.

"Yes—these are the subtle signs: like a night scene illumined by a flash of lightning, they may be revealed to

24

you for but an instant. And these Worlds of Spirit may not fully open to you at once. But you will never, ever after, be able to doubt their existence."

Riding the Wave

"How can I find stability in the flow of life? Where is the resting place?" lamented the Daughter.

"We necessarily live our life as a *Wave of possibility*—knowing that such open potential will finally collapse into an Event. This describes the nature of all Reality as well."

"Where is Freedom then, if we are merely carried along?"

"We act, as well, in our human response. But our strength is to be found in endurance, in riding our course confidently to its end."

* * *

"But all 'events' will not be to our liking. How do we know we are not sailing toward disaster?" the Daughter continued.

"All we can know is that we live in a World worthy of singing about—*and* weeping over."

* * *

"But what of the years of sorrow—how can the quantity of our grief, and that of all the world, ever be contained? Surely it would fill an ocean," the Daughter protested.

"Tears are the 'Philosopher's Wine,'" said her Mother. "Yet even in their bitterness they can nourish and sustain. All plants need water."

* * *

"But we are not as the plants are—we have our own

'field'—our Work."

"The 'Field' stands for the group of conditions and possibilities contained within corporeality," the Mother explained. "Here within our humanness lies the potential for many forms and Patterns to grow and thrive. 'For we are workers with God: you are God's planting, God's building.'"[9]

* * *

"How can we ever expect that our human plans, our efforts, will get it right?"

"Divine guidance is like one moon shining in 100 bowls of water," the Mother mused. "Love comes down, and we reflect back Love in return. This alone should be our aim in all we do."

* * *

"Mother, how do you know these things? Will I in turn learn how to read signs and happenings?"

"Nothing is covered that will not be revealed, or hidden that will not be known,"[10] her Mother answered. "For those who are truly seeking in the light of Love, all shall be Well."

* * *

"At night my Soul searches in ways it cannot during the day. What is the meaning of those experiences? Is nothing of them 'real'?"

"Dreams are like the sun shining in the middle of the night," the Mother said. "We need all available Lights to see the map before us and follow it."

* * *

"How will I know I am on the right Path, especially when it winds through a dark woods?"

"When blind eyes see, deaf ears hear, and the thick tongue speaks with clear words. These were the everyday miracles of which Jesus spoke.[11] We too will see such impossible things happen," her Mother assured her. "That is the Path we would be on."

* * *

"What if I stumble, or miss the clues that are before my eyes?" the Daughter worried aloud.

"Life is about finding for yourself the trustworthy thread of Ariadne, so that you can wend your way Home. You will know what is Gold when all else is revealed to you as straw."

Weaving Gold

"What is the nature of that thread that I must grasp and follow?"

"It is *Compassion* that connects us, both as a force in the material realm and as an earthly taste of the Divine," her Mother said. "Cherish it in your Heart and take it with you always."

* * *

"How can we acquire this 'Gold' to work with that will provide us a link from this world to the next?"

"This is the question of the Ages. All we can do is continue to weave honest lives through our choices before God day to day. This journeying is also a picture of the Soul's reaching toward that World," her Mother said.

* * *

"The days sift through my hands, and I feel I cannot grasp what needs to be done before it fades and is lost. This makes me fearful of tomorrow."

"Do not fear, as fear crowds out Love," said the Mother, hugging her Daughter. "It is only through fearless engagement in the world we inhabit that we can grow to participate freely in what lies beyond this realm."

* * *

"I want to be a revealer of Spirit in the world—to give back to the Universe from the riches that have been strewn at my feet."

"Your rays shine out!" Her Mother smiled. "Daily you immerse yourself in the stream of the Word, and of the lives of Wise Ones who have gone before. As you follow this Path, in a Mystery, *you are making it your own.*"

* * *

"What can you teach me of this World, while I am still with you and Father in this Home?"

"Look to emptiness as well as fullness. It is necessary to be at home with openness, to allow a space for Spirit to fill. This practice is also known as *Obedience*—as Mary proclaimed, 'I am your handmaid.'"

* * *

"Mother, I feel so close to you, as though sometimes in our Work—and play—our hearts beat as one," the Daughter admitted.

"Souls 'of a feather' will always be closely twined in some sense, no matter how great their distance in miles. This Truth gives me great joy as well!"

* * *

"Will I always need such close instruction, and hands-on guidance?" the Daughter asked.

"The wise Mother works herself gradually out of a job..."

* * *

"Will I ever 'get it'? The world of Knowledge lies before me, and yet I know so little of it. I am ever starting again at the beginning," the Daughter lamented.

"But that is the best place to be—at the Beginning. The important thing is 'knowing how to know.' *Ask, seek, knock,* as Jesus said. And never cease."

* * *

"Sometimes we are so busy, and the Work presses us so, I almost forget to breathe!" the Daughter admitted.

"Yet, just as breathing is our 'second food,' so is *seeking* second nature to our Soul. When you 'forget' you are breathing or seeking, your true nature as a child of God is still operating. Sometimes it is better to be 'invisible' to ourselves."

* * *

"Still, something in me laments: *O that life were more than its fragments!* When will I know the 'whole'?"

"Just as you cannot rush the living of your life, and must take one moment at a time, so the particulars from which you build daily are adding up to more than you realize. Someday you will have 'eyes to see.'"

* * *

"But it is so difficult to wait, and I want that Fullness now..."

"As the great Jacob Boehme has said, 'Heaven is hidden in the heart,'" her Mother reminded her. "When you search and know your own Gold, there you will find it."

* * *

"How can we know with certainty that God is with us in the spinning and the weaving of our lives?"

The Mother looked into her Daughter's lovely eyes. "Though we should rightly be unaware of it, others may acknowledge that the Face of all faces can, from time to time, be seen reflected in our own."

* * *

"Every day I learn something new, even in the tasks that have become second-nature to my hands," the Daughter exulted as she found her stitching improved.

"Just so, chasing Truth, like opening a succession of smaller and smaller Russian dolls, eventually reveals the kernel we were seeking."

* * *

"What IS the drive that keeps me working, learning, finding?"

"At every point of comprehension," her Mother explained, "one is automatically attracted to the next, more complex principle. The thread of Ariadne is not only a vehicle of rescue, but also a lifeline pulling us from one level to the next."

"It is sometimes more than I can bear, this constant pulling," the Daughter said.

"We cling to Spirit for Life—and the Life we are granted enables us to hold on, in a paradox."

* * *

"Mother, what truly is Real in this world, and how can we know it?"

"*To love* means to affirm something to be present in the full measure of its Reality," her Mother explained. "You and your Father are the most Real to me, and I discover and know you both anew every day."

* * *

"What IS the burden of Love, and how do we bear it?" the Daughter asked, her heart full to the brim.

"Love teaches us the weight and worth of Gold. No gift comes without cost. When one you love suffers, you feel that heaviness. Yet you would never surrender the Gold that comes with the bearing of its burden."

* * *

"What is our Purpose here, and for what ends do we strive all these workdays of our lives?" the Daughter asked one day at sundown.

"As St. Catherine of Siena wisely told us, 'Make two homes for thyself, my daughter. One actual home...and the other a spiritual home, which thou are to carry with thee always.' These are the two lives we are building as we labor, sometimes all in one motion."

* * *

The Daughter asked, "Can our actions in the present truly reach back—and even change the nature of the Past?"

"In a Mystery, Time's arrow does indeed stretch both ways. See the careful and minute stitches we are taking even now, each in its succession? Just so, each act helps determine whether this Life we are working on has been a garment of Joy from the beginning."

* * *

"Could we really learn to spin straw into 'Gold'?" the Daughter asked playfully.

"To be able to create Gold, one first has to *have* Gold. And those who *do* need not ask!"

* * *

"What IS the purpose of straw in our lives? Why could we not just be given pure Gold, have perfect lives from the beginning?"

"But it would render all our work meaningless, if we had all that we seek from the start. Savor the journey, my Child—learn and grow along with those you love. This is the Way that God has called us to live. And then, looking back, even what was 'straw' will seem to glow in surprising ways to your Heart."

* * *

The Mother called an end to the day's labor, putting away her own half-finished work, folding materials and covering the spindles.

"Could we not continue until the Light fades more?"

"Yes, my Daughter. But just as the threads fragilely connect one day to the next, and our hands can only work artfully for so many hours—we will not *cease*, but only *turn*—and continue our efforts in ongoing Love."

Afterword

"Begin to weave and God will give you the thread." — German proverb.

What are our lives as women to be about? The answers may be as simple and as close to us as what our hands find to do (cf. Ecclesiastes 9:10).

Though actual spinning and weaving may not be our gift, there are always lessons to be learned in acceptance of our given materials (Virginia Woolf urged us to "Arrange whatever pieces come your way")—and in what we make of them.

"What we have loved, others will love, and we will teach them how." —Wordsworth.

"Beauty is the promise of happiness." —Henri B. Stendhal.

"In the evening of life, we will be judged on love alone." —St. John of the Cross, Christian mystic and poet (1542–1591).

Notes

1 From *Rilke's Book of Hours: Love Poems to God,* by Rainer Maria Rilke, translated by Anita Barrows and Joanna Macy. New York: Riverhead Books, 1996, p. 64. Used by permission.

2 *Receiving Woman* (Philadelphia: Westminster Press, 1981), p. 158.

3 L. Maloney in *The Lost Coin: Parables of Women, Work, and Wisdom* by Mary Ann Beavis; New York: Continuum, 2002), p. 24.

4 *The Medieval Woman* (Boston: Little, Brown and Company, 1985).

5 Psalm 139:13.

6 Proverbs 14:1.

7 Genesis 28:15.

8 Sirach 38:34.

9 1 Corinthians 3:9.

10 Matthew 10:26.

11 Luke 7:22.

Questions for Study Groups

1. How would you describe the shape of the life that you are weaving in this world? What do its parameters and texture and quality say to those around you, especially the people that you love?

2. We can evaluate our lives in terms of materials, methods, time, intentions, and results, much as we would an artistic or utilitarian project or work. If you were able to change any of these elements, how would your life unfold differently? Which factors are within your power to change or to view differently? What actions will you take in the light of this evaluation?

3. In what ways do you consider your own work "spiritual" and even eternal in its value and permanence? How does this insight influence the way you go about working and living among the persons given you to love?

4. How does cultural language used toward and against women affect your sense of self, and how can you personally contribute to the building up and recognition of feminine strength, value, and beauty in the world?

5. Has your view of *time* changed as you have matured? How is time both a taskmaster and a friend in a woman's journey toward wisdom and fulfillment?

6. In what ways have dialogues with other women (and with men) aided you in your spiritual journey? How have you learned to listen to more than words, to context and tone and feelings conveyed? How can women help men to learn and practice these listening skills?

7. What works of literature, both "holy" and practical,

have been your guides and support in your journey? How can a reconsideration of traditional wisdom help to illuminate a post-modern life? How can the ancient/biblical "way of wisdom" still work in our world today?

8. What do you seek? What is your heart gently telling you in silence and solitude? How will you respond?

9. What steps do you need to take that you may have been putting off until your life reaches another stage of development or maturity? How can you prepare for these anticipated changes while you are still in your present circumstances?

10. The biblical Apostle John was said to have repeated at the end of his life only this admonition: "Little children, love one another!" How is love "all we need" and also just the beginning of a life that spins straw into gold?

Bibliography

Beavis, Mary Ann. *The Lost Coin: Parables of Women, Work, and Wisdom.* New York: Continuum, 2002.

Fox, Sally. *The Medieval Woman.* Boston: Little, Brown and Company, 1985.

Shapiro, Rabbi Rami. *The Divine Feminine in Biblical Wisdom Literature.* Woodstock, Vermont: Skylight Paths Publishing, 2005.

Ulanov, Ann Belford. *Receiving Woman.* Philadelphia: Westminster Press, 1981.

Circle Books

Circle is a symbol of infinity and unity. It's part of a growing list of imprints, including o-books.net and zero-books.net.

Circle Books aims to publish books in Christian spirituality that are fresh, accessible, and stimulating.

Our books are available in all good English language bookstores worldwide. If you can't find the book on the shelves, then ask your bookstore to order it for you, quoting the ISBN and title. Or, you can order online—all major online retail sites carry our titles.

To see our list of titles, please view www.Circle-Books.com, growing by 80 titles per year.

Authors can learn more about our proposal process by going to our website and clicking on Your Company > Submissions.

We define Christian spirituality as the relationship between the self and its sense of the transcendent or sacred, which issues in literary and artistic expression, community, social activism, and practices. A wide range of disciplines within the field of religious studies can be called upon, including history, narrative studies, philosophy, theology, sociology, and psychology. Interfaith in approach, Circle Books fosters creative dialogue with non-Christian traditions.

And tune into MySpiritRadio.com for our book review radio show, hosted by June-Elleni Laine, where you can listen to authors discussing their books.

MySpiritRadio